TWISTING THE TRUTH

PARTICIPANT'S GUIDE

Andy Stanley

ZONDERVAN®

NORTH POINT
RESOURCES

ZONDERVAN.com/
AUTHORTRACKER
follow your favorite authors

ZONDERVAN®

Twisting the Truth Participant's Guide
Copyright © 2008 by North Point Ministries, Inc.

Requests for information should be addressed to:
Zondervan, *Grand Rapids, Michigan 49530*

ISBN 978-0-310-28766-7

Cover and interior design by Brian Manley (funwithrobots.com)

Printed in the United States of America

17 18 • 23 22 21 20 19 18 17

CONTENTS

INTRODUCTION

INVISIBLE WORLD

by Andy Stanley

You know how amazingly weird it is — moments of clarity followed suddenly by moments of insanity. We may know the right thing to do; yet we go out and do the exact opposite.

Why's that? Is something wrong with us?

Or could it be there's an invisible world impacting our visible world? Is there something we can't see influencing everything we can see?

The Bible's answer is that, yes, there's an unseen world affecting our lives. It's all around us. It impacts every single thing we do, everything about us. It affects all our relationships. It influences our thinking, our attitudes, our decision-making. It colors our perspectives on finances, on morality, and on how we do business. And it can actually be life-threatening — physically, emotionally, and relationally.

Hard to Accept

Many of us find this idea a bit difficult to accept. But the same Bible that tells us things we enjoy hearing — like "Love one another" and "God so loved the world" — that same Bible makes clear the existence of this invisible world.

Still, as we learn more about it and face up to it, we often tend to resist this concept. We're like some people in the 1800s who had trouble accepting the amazing new scientific discoveries of an entire world of microorganisms living all around us, invisible to the naked eye yet affecting all of human life.

The invisible world taught in the Bible isn't one you need a microscope to discover. All you need is a rearview mirror — a glance at your past. I can look back on moments in my life and say, "How could I have been so stupid, so confused? How could I have thought that was a good thing when now I recognize it so clearly as a bad thing? How could my thinking get so twisted?"

We can all look back on certain times — a night, a weekend, seasons in our lives — and feel that way.

Why in the world did I think that relationship was going anywhere good?

Why did I think that approach to finances would bring anything but disaster?

Yet at the moment, it made perfect sense. We talked ourselves into things we knew we had no business doing.

It's not that we want to mess up our lives. But in certain environments or with certain groups of people, it's like we lose our minds. We're in some kind of fog. We miss all the warnings.

How can we be so deceived?

With Others Too

The same mystery shows itself when you look around at people you love, people you want the best for. Even when it's so clear to you (and everybody who knows them) that they're making terrible decisions, they push ahead anyway. You think, *Why can't they see this like I see it?* Yet for them it makes total sense, and they have no trouble stating their cases — their logic is so fouled up, their thinking so twisted. Only later will they wonder, *What was I thinking?*

The Bible tells us why we experience this. It's because there's a twistedness all around us — a distortion of truth, twisted just enough to draw us into trouble, but not quite enough to scare us away.

And the ones behind this twist will never tip their hands. If they became too obvious, we'd see them for who they are — and we'd run.

Seeing Through It

Interestingly, not everybody falls for these twists. Some people (although, let's face it, they're the exceptions) are somehow able to navigate these minefields and see through the deceit. They've learned not to make so many bad decisions. They live differently. They do work and relationships and marriage and family differently. They don't buy into our culture's definition of how to handle morality, how to handle money, how to view the world. They do it all another way.

They're just so different. And in our moments of sanity, we think, *I want to be like that.*

Again, they're the exceptions, not the rule. But — can we somehow take hold of what they've learned?

Let's find out.

THE SOURCE OF DECEPTION

Doctors and scientists once believed that diseases just "popped up" spontaneously with no explainable cause.

Then, in the 1800s, Louis Pasteur and others confirmed the presence of invisible organisms that carried disease. These microorganisms can be found everywhere — in the air, in our food, and on all kinds of surfaces. They represent an invisible world constantly impacting the visible world, bringing infection and illness and even death.

The Bible tells us about another unseen world that constantly impacts us in harmful ways. Jesus gives us specific insight into it, and his explanation is unsettling, almost disturbing.

But maybe it can also be helpful. Maybe it explains some things. Maybe it's something we need to learn to factor into our struggles with temptation and in our difficulties in relationships and in marriage and in our families.

DISCUSSION STARTER

Talk about a time in the past when you were deceived by someone, or you fell for some hoax or trick. What was the reason behind the deception? Could you have avoided it? If so, how?

In general, how susceptible to deception do you consider yourself to be?

VIDEO OVERVIEW

FOR SESSION 1 OF THE DVD

In the gospel of John, we get Jesus' take on an unseen world. He was having a conversation with religious leaders who refused to recognize who he was, although his words and actions proved that he'd come from God. Jesus let them know why they were unable to recognize him: "Why is my language not clear to you? Because you are unable to hear what I say. *You belong to your father, the devil,* and you want to carry out your father's desire" (John 8:43–44).

Jesus went on to describe the devil this way: *"He was a murderer* from the beginning, not holding to the truth, for there is no truth in him. When he lies, he speaks his native language, for *he is a liar* and the father of lies" (8:44).

Jesus was saying, "Why don't you get it? It's because there's a deceiver, the devil, the source and originator of all lies. And you've been so influenced by his power that your thinking is too twisted to recognize me."

So Jesus believed in the personal existence of the devil, whose ultimate agenda was the destruction of human life and whose tool is deception — distorting and twisting truth. He can persuade human beings that what's right is wrong and what's wrong is right. It devastates our hearts and minds, and sometimes even our bodies. It wrecks relationships, marriages, families, and anything that's truly valuable to the human race.

Jesus later referred to the devil as "the prince of this world" (John 12:31 and 14:30). This corresponds to an earlier confrontation between Jesus and the devil. Having come to tempt Jesus, the devil "led him up to a high place and showed him in an instant *all the kingdoms of the world.* And he said to him, 'I will give you *all their authority and splendor,* for *it has been given to me,* and I can give it to anyone I want to'" (Luke 4:5–6).

In an important sense, our world is currently the devil's domain, where he has been given authority to use deception in trying to accomplish his destructive agenda.

Scary, isn't it? But maybe it helps explain the intensity of our struggles with temptation and our inconsistency in doing what we know — in our saner moments — is right. Something invisible is impacting everything we do and see.

VIDEO NOTES

_____

_____

_____

_____

_____

_____

_____

_____

_____

_____

_____

_____

_____

_____

_____

_____

_____

_____

_____

DISCUSSION QUESTIONS

1. In what ways are you affected by things you can't see (e.g., germs, electricity, the wind)?

2. How does our culture portray the devil?

3. What is your understanding of who the devil is?

4. What do we learn about the devil from Jesus in John 8:43–44?

5. Read Luke 4:5–6. Does it surprise you that God has granted the devil temporary influence on the world around us? Why would God allow this?

6. How has the devil's influence been felt in this world?

MILEPOSTS

- The Bible assures us of the devil's existence and that this world is under his influence.
- The devil is a murderer, and his agenda is the destruction of human life and all that is good in human life.
- To accomplish this agenda, the devil's tool is *deception*. He is a liar and the source and originator of lies.

MOVING FORWARD

We read in the gospel of John that shortly before Jesus was arrested and crucified, he twice referred to the devil as "the prince of this world." Yet Jesus didn't say the devil had either total control or final victory. Instead he said, "Now the prince of this world *will be driven out*" (12:31), and, "The prince of this world is coming. *He has no hold on me*" (14:30). What specific assurance and confidence do these statements give you about the power that we have through Jesus to resist the devil? What difference could this make in your own view of the devil? Write out the most important things you need to remember about what you've just learned.

CHANGING YOUR MIND

It's easy to lose perspective on what the devil is really like — and the danger this brings into our daily lives. You can become more aware of this by meditating on the following verse this week. Remember that this description of the devil comes directly from Jesus:

He was a murderer from the beginning,
not holding to the truth,
for there is no truth in him.
When he lies, he speaks his native language,
for he is a liar and the father of lies.

John 8:44

PREPARATION FOR SESSION 2

To help you prepare for Session 2, use these suggested devotions during the week leading up to your small group meeting.

Day One

Review the words of Jesus in John 8:42–44. As you reflect further on these truths about the devil and how he operates, how do you see his strategy being played out in our lives and in our world today?

Day Two

Read Ephesians 6:10–11. As Paul encourages us to become "strong in the Lord," what reason does he give? What dangers does he say are out there? And why do you think these dangers require us to "put on the full armor of God"?

Day Three

Read Ephesians 6:12. Paul acknowledges that we face a "struggle." Who is it *not* with? Who does Paul say our true struggle is against, and what does that mean to you?

Day Four

Read again Ephesians 6:10–12. Do you think there's any way to avoid the struggle Paul mentions here? If so, how? Or, if it's unavoidable, what's the best response we can aim for? Is this somehow better than avoiding the struggle entirely? If so, why and how?

Day Five

Read Ephesians 6:13–18. As we face this struggle with the devil, what resources from God — what "armor" — can we use and depend on? What do these mean practically to you?

Last Session

We saw the warning from Jesus that the devil is a murderer, and that his agenda is the destruction of human life and everything that's good to us. He's also a liar. To accomplish his agenda, his chief tool is *deception*.

ALL IS NOT AS IT SEEMS

When Jesus accused the religious leaders (in John 8) of belonging to the devil — whom he called "a murderer" and "a liar" — he was foreshadowing a tragic fact: These same religious leaders, under the devil's deceptive influence, would soon murder Jesus by plotting to have him crucified.

The invisible world would do its work. Deception would lead to death, fulfilling the devil's destructive agenda.

About thirty years later, the apostle Paul showed how fully he understood what Jesus had taught about this invisible world. Paul was writing letters of instruction and counsel to Christians in the new churches scattered across the Roman Empire, teaching them about their relationships and their conduct and how to live. He told them what *not* to do and what to do. And he emphasized the dangers coming our way from this unseen world.

DISCUSSION STARTER

What is something that you have heard lately that was twisted? What is something that was true that someone took and twisted for his or her purpose?

VIDEO OVERVIEW

FOR SESSION 2 OF THE DVD

In his letter to Christians in Ephesus, Paul told them, "Put on the full armor of God so that you can take your stand against *the devil's schemes*" (Ephesians 6:11).

Paul, who wrote much of the New Testament, believed that there is a devil — an individual personality — who has *schemes*. And the devil's strategy behind those schemes is simple: Take what's true, and twist it. Take what's evident, and distort it. Change it just enough to lead people astray.

For example: Our appetites are good things, but the devil twists them to where they become addictions. He twists our desires and our appreciation into things like greed and jealousy and lust. And he twists people's views of God so that they get angry at him, make rash decisions in their anger — then blame God for the consequences.

The devil has schemes, plans, a strategy. And when you begin factoring this into your own experience, there's a lot to learn.

Paul goes on to say, "For our struggle is not against flesh and blood, but against the rulers, against the authorities, against the powers of this dark world and against the spiritual forces of evil in the heavenly realms" (Ephesians 6:12).

Our struggle is not against flesh and blood. This is so helpful when you're in the middle of some relational issue. It's not just your spouse that's the problem. It's not just your daughter or your son that's the problem. It's not just your boss or your coworker that's the problem. It's not just you that's the problem. Paul is telling us, "Remember to factor this in: It's not just what you see. What you see is being impacted by an invisible realm — dark powers, spiritual forces of evil."

You may be skeptical about this. If so, that's understandable. After all, it's invisible! Besides, we tend to have our own explanations for the struggles and troubles people get into.

But every once in a while, we see something or hear about something or read about something — senseless shootings, child prostitution, terrorist acts, genocide — and we think, *That's just evil.* That's the only explanation. Ultimately it can't be explained without factoring in the devil — the schemer and deceiver.

VIDEO NOTES

_____

_____

_____

_____

_____

_____

_____

_____

_____

_____

_____

_____

_____

_____

_____

_____

_____

_____

_____

_____

DISCUSSION QUESTIONS

1. From your observations, how has our world been affected by twisted thinking?

2. How have you fallen victim to twisted thinking in the past? Are there times when you've looked back and asked, "What was I thinking?" How were you led astray?

3. If it's not because of an evil entity called the devil, how do people account for twisted thinking?

4. Read Ephesians 6:12. Do you agree that we struggle not only against what we can see, but also against unseen forces? How does this fact affect some of the current conflicts you're experiencing?

5. According to Ephesians 6:13–17, how can you protect yourself from twisted thinking?

MILEPOSTS

- The devil's destructive and deceptive strategy includes many schemes that attempt to twist the truth.
- Though the devil is invisible, his destructive campaign against us inevitably brings struggle into our lives.
- The degree of evil we see in our world is a compelling argument for the devil's destructive and deceptive power.

MOVING FORWARD

As you more clearly recognize the power and influence of the devil's deceptions, Proverbs 30:8 is a good prayer: "Keep falsehood and lies far from me." Another good request to pray regularly is this: "God, help me see as you see."

Now, think about the most important struggles or difficulties you're facing. They may include temptations to sin, as well as difficulties in your marriage, family, other relationships, finances, or work. Think about what you've learned in Sessions 1 and 2 regarding the devil and his opposition to us. How should that influence your perspective on your personal struggles? Write out the most important things you need to remember about what you've just learned.

CHANGING YOUR MIND

God's Word is full of reality checks about our lives. The following passage is one of them. Meditate on it this week, using it as a reminder of our true enemy.

> *Put on the full armor of God so that you can take your stand*
> *against the devil's schemes.*
> *For our struggle is not against flesh and blood,*
> *but against the rulers, against the authorities,*
> *against the powers of this dark world*
> *and against the spiritual forces of evil in the heavenly realms.*

Ephesians 6:11–12

PREPARATION FOR SESSION 3

To help you prepare for Session 3, use these suggested devotions during the week leading up to your small group meeting.

Day One

One of the devil's biggest twists has to do with authority. Read Romans 13:1. What response to "governing authorities" are we told to have, and what does it involve? What reason for this response does Paul give? What's the most important element in how God wants us to view governing authorities?

Day Two

Read Romans 13:2–3. What are some common ways in which we might "rebel against…authority"? Why is this the same as rebellion against God? What's the easiest way to avoid trouble — and God's judgment — in this area? And what would that mean in practical terms in your life?

Day Three

Read Romans 13:4. What description is given twice in this verse for someone in authority? And what is the purpose of this authority, in God's eyes? Does this description apply to all human authorities? Why or why not?

Day Four

Read Romans 13:5. Paul gives two reasons here for submitting to authority. What are they? Is it enough to obey authorities just to stay out of trouble? What do you think goes into having a clear conscience with regard to authorities that are over us?

Day Five

Read Romans 13:6–7. Paul mentions here a specific aspect of submitting to authorities. Is this particular area one that you have a clear conscience about? Also, Paul here repeats a description of authorities that he gave twice in verse 4. What is it? Why do you think it's so important for us to have this perspective about human authorities?

Last Session

We learned about the devil's deceptive schemes: his attempt to twist the truth that inevitably bring struggles into our lives.

In the remaining sessions of this study, we'll look at some of the biggest twists from the devil that impact all of us — bringing confusion in our decision-making, in our relationships, in the way we think about morality and ethics, and in the way we go about our everyday lives. The twist we will cover in Session 3 has to do with authority.

SESSION 3

SAYS WHO?

Authority. Teenagers love to rebel against authority. In their minds, rebellion equals freedom. That's the basic premise we've operated from since we were about twelve or thirteen, right? It made sense: *The best path to freedom is to forget the rules.*

As we grew up, it morphed into something more sophisticated. After all, we came to realize that prisons are full of people who lost their freedom because they rebelled. And we're smarter than that.

So our revised adult version of rebellion goes like this: *I'll just ignore any particular rule I disagree with.* Instead of a blanket dismissal of all authority, we take it one rule at a time. If we don't like it — if we think it's irrelevant or stupid or antiquated or extreme — we disregard it.

We do it all the time.

- A 45-mph speed limit on this road? *That's ridiculous.* We drive 60.

- It's tax return time. *This ought to be a deduction; it's just common sense.* The IRS may not allow it, but we'll deduct it anyway.

- There's a rule in the company's policy manual that we find impractical. And we don't see anyone else following it. So we don't either.

Is this really *rebellion*? And if so ... against whom?

DISCUSSION STARTER

Remember back to a time in your youth (or later) when you rebelled against some rule or authority. How did you express or carry out this rebellion? How did you arrive at the decision to disregard this rule or authority? What were your most important assumptions about authority in general? And how have those assumptions changed over time?

VIDEO OVERVIEW

FOR SESSION 3 OF THE DVD

The issue of authority is really where it all began — going all the way back to the garden of Eden.

Here's the twist: When it comes to authority, our first response is to evaluate the *what.* If someone— parents, teachers, our bosses, the government, or whomever — is telling us what to do, our first reaction is to make a judgment about what's being asked or required of us. And if it doesn't meet our approval, we disregard it — without any guilt.

Or we might go along with it only to avoid unpleasant consequences — *not* from any genuine submission to authority. But as long as we can get away with ignoring any rule or regulation we don't like, that's what we do.

This is a huge twist that impacts us deeply and at multiple levels.

The Scriptures unmask this twist. When it comes to authority, God tells us, "No, it's not about *what;* it's about *who.*"

Paul speaks to this issue in Romans 13. This letter to Christians in Rome was written when the tyrant Nero was emperor. His rule was oppressive, and Christians were persecuted. Yet Paul told them, "Everyone must submit himself to the governing authorities, for *there is no authority except that which God has established.* The authorities that exist have been established by God" (Romans 13:1).

He emphasizes a principle that we find throughout the Scriptures: *God works through human authority.* Through all human authority — good and bad, righteous and unrighteous, believing and unbelieving — he's at work to exercise his will on the earth.

Paul then writes, "Consequently, he who rebels against the authority is rebelling against what God has instituted, and those who do so will bring judgment on themselves" (13:2). To rebel against authorities such as parents, teachers, employers, or the government is ultimately to rebel against God. For as Paul says, each human authority in your life "is God's servant to do you good" (13:4).

Our attitudes and responses toward human authorities is therefore a reflection of our attitudes and responses to our Father in heaven. When we resist the authorities he has placed over us, we're also resisting God.

VIDEO NOTES

_____

_____

_____

_____

_____

_____

_____

_____

_____

_____

_____

_____

_____

_____

_____

_____

_____

_____

DISCUSSION QUESTIONS

1. What rules or regulations do you disagree with? Do you
   follow them or ignore them?

2. What determines whether or not you submit to authority
   and follow the rules?

3. Does it surprise you that, according to Romans 13:1, *all*
   authorities have been set up by God? How about the authorities who don't follow God?

4. What is at stake when we choose to rebel?

5. What is the purpose of authority? Why not live in a world
   with no rules or hierarchy?

6. What are some ways that you could experience more freedom by submitting to authority?

MILEPOSTS

- Our natural response to authority is to evaluate everything
  we're asked to do, then do only to what we agree with.
- The Bible teaches us that God has established human authorities as agents of his own will.
- To rebel against the human authorities God has established
  is ultimately to rebel against God himself.

MOVING FORWARD

God's design for following authority actually gives you the opportunity to experience more freedom, not less. Have you thought of ways in which you haven't been fully submitting to an authority God has placed over you? If so, what changes do you need to make immediately? Write out the steps of action you'll take to correct this.

CHANGING YOUR MIND

Our responses toward human authority tend to be so different from what God intends. That's why it's good to meditate on this week's verses. Consider writing out these words and keeping them with you to look over often as you let their truth saturate your mind.

Everyone must submit himself to the governing authorities,
for there is no authority except that which God has established.
The authorities that exist have been established by God.
Consequently, he who rebels against the authority
is rebelling against what God has instituted,
and those who do so will bring judgment on themselves.

Romans 13:1–2

PREPARATION FOR SESSION 4

To help you prepare for Session 4, use these suggested devotions during the week leading up to your small group meeting.

Day One

Another of the devil's deceptions has to do with suffering. Read Romans 8:18–21. In these words to Christians in Rome, how does Paul urge us to view our present sufferings in light of our *past,* our *present,* and our *future*? What are the negatives that are talked about here? And what are the positives?

Day Two

Read Romans 8:22–23. What does Paul say is true about our *present* and about our *future*? What are believers in Christ waiting for? Paul mentions something that's going to be redeemed — what is it? If it's not yet redeemed, what is its condition now? (Refer back also to verses 18–21.)

Day Three

Read Romans 8:24–25. What exactly is "hope"? What's your understanding of it? What seems to be Paul's understanding of it? What attitudes and responses does true hope produce in our lives?

Day Four

Read Romans 8:26–27. What specific help can we count on from God's Spirit? Why does Paul say we need this help? What words in this passage do you personally identify with most?

Day Five

Read Romans 8:28. What does Paul want us to understand about ourselves? What does he want us to understand about God? What does he want us to understand about our circumstances?

Last Session

We saw that our twisted response to authority is to always evaluate the *what* before choosing to submit. But God says it's all about the *who*, not the what. In other words, God is behind all human authority, and not to submit to that authority is to rebel against God. This week we will turn to the twist that has been placed on our pain.

SESSION 4

FACING FORWARD

"God whispers to us in our pleasures, speaks in our conscience, but shouts in our pains," wrote C. S. Lewis; *"it is His megaphone to rouse a deaf world."*

Experiencing pain and suffering, more than anything else, brings us face to face with God. When the bottom drops out and things go terribly wrong, our inclination is to look upward. And the question we usually ask is this: *Why, God?* Why me? Why him? Why her, when she's so young? Why now? Why this? Why would you let it happen again?

Knowing the answers won't make the pain go away. But we feel that if somehow we can make sense out of what's happened, if we can just see that this is leading to something good, we'll find it easier to endure the pain and loss and suffering. *There must be some purpose to my pain.*

So we immediately try to piece things together. What did I do to cause this? If only I'd paid closer attention … worked harder … been a better friend … a better husband … a better parent.

Somehow, we've got to connect the dots.

DISCUSSION STARTER

What is something that has happened to you in the past few weeks that has caused you pain?

VIDEO OVERVIEW

FOR SESSION 4 OF THE DVD

In Romans 8, Paul takes us through the history of human suffering. He connects three big dots — "in the beginning," "in the meantime," and "in the end."

In the beginning . . .

Taking us back to "in the beginning," he reminds us that sin entered the world, bringing death and God's judgment. Ever since humankind's first sin, the world has been cursed; sin reigns and continues to have its ruinous way. "The creation was subjected to frustration" (Romans 8:20), Paul tells us, with that word *frustration* implying depravity and perversion.

Therefore "creation itself" is in "bondage to decay" (8:21). We're all under this bondage. We've been set up for struggle.

When suffering and difficulties come your way, it's not just a breakdown in your personal well-being; it's a reflection of *the whole world being broken.* It's not simply that your family or marriage or career or health is broken; *everything around us has always been broken.* We're *born* broken.

That's why things go wrong, our plans don't work out, expectations aren't met. The world is in a broken state, and none of us is exempt. Under that burden, "the whole creation has been groaning as in the pains of childbirth right up to the present time" (8:22). For the present — "in the meantime" — we groan from daily experiencing the effects of sin and decay.

The whole world is broken

In the meantime

In the end . . .

But Paul also points us toward to the future — "in the end." He tells us, "Creation itself will be *liberated* ... and brought into the glorious freedom of the children of God" (8:21). As believers in Christ, this soon-coming future will mean "our adoption as sons" and *"redemption"* — not just of our souls, but "of our bodies" (8:23).

Therefore Paul can say, "I consider that our present sufferings are not worth comparing with the glory that will be revealed in us" (8:18).

In the meantime . . .

So our present experience can be filled with hope. "We hope for what we do not yet have," Paul says, which means "we wait for it patiently" (8:25). We can lean forward eagerly, awaiting the ultimate redemption of our bodies, when our salvation is complete.

To get us through, "the Spirit helps us in our weakness" (8:26). It's normal to feel weak and frustrated, "but the Spirit himself intercedes for us with groans that words cannot express" (8:26). God fully understands our situation, and his Spirit is praying for us "in accordance with God's will" (8:27).

VIDEO NOTES

DISCUSSION QUESTIONS

1. Why do we tend to believe the twist that the reason for our pain can be found in past events or present circumstances?

2. When have you tried to do this only to end up frustrated? That is, when have you experienced pain, or watched as others experienced pain, that seemed to have no purpose?

3. According to Romans 8:18, we are to hold our present suffering in light of a more hopeful future. But how has the pain in your life affected your present relationship with God? Has it made you more dependent on him? Or has it pushed you away and made you more independent? How have you seen suffering affect the faith of those around you?

4. In the beginning, God created a paradise (Genesis 1); however, when we rebelled, sin, death, and decay entered the world (Genesis 3). How does "the beginning" relate to your understanding of the pain you've experienced?

5. Romans 8:26–27 addresses the Spirit's work in our weakness. How does the Spirit help us "in the meantime"? How does God provide help for us during times of suffering?

6. How does knowing what lies ahead in "the end" affect our present suffering?

MILEPOSTS

- We live with a broken world that's in bondage to sin, death, and decay — all as a result of humanity's first rebellion against God.
- In this life we cannot escape the effects of sin, death, and decay. In many ways, life on this earth will always be a downward spiral.
- But we can look forward in hope to a future when we'll experience complete liberation and salvation. Meanwhile, God helps us in our weakness as we wait eagerly for what's ahead.

MOVING FORWARD

For now, God promises us his presence, his comfort, and the prayers of the Holy Spirit on our behalf. But there lies a future when God will bring a complete end to all human pain and suffering. Paul speaks in Romans 8 about a future so glorious that "our present sufferings are not worth comparing" with it. He talks about the "hope" we can have as we "wait patiently" for these things. How much are you hoping for such things in your eternal future? How patiently are you waiting for them? How real is your hope? Write an assessment of your heart and mind on these issues.

CHANGING YOUR MIND

Meditating on the following verses from Romans 8 can help us keep an "in the end" focus — while "in the meantime" we rely on the Holy Spirit's help — as we encounter suffering because of what happened to humanity "in the beginning."

> *I consider that our present sufferings are not worth comparing*
> *with the glory that will be revealed in us....*
> *The Spirit helps us in our weakness.*
> *We do not know what we ought to pray for,*
> *but the Spirit himself intercedes for us*
> *with groans that words cannot express.*
>
> *Romans 8:18, 26*

PREPARATION FOR SESSION 5

To help you prepare for Session 5, use these suggested devotions during the week leading up to your small group meeting.

Day One

The devil has done much to twist sex in our culture. Read 1 Corinthians 6:13. Paul mentions "sexual immorality" here. From what you know of the Bible, how do you think Paul would define this term? Do you think the Bible's definition is the same as your definition for "sexual immorality"? In pointing us away from sexual immorality in this verse, what truth does Paul point us *toward?*

Day Two

Read 1 Corinthians 6:18. What basic response does Paul say we should have toward sexual immorality? Is sexual sin in a category all its own? If so, why? What's different about it?

Day Three

Read 1 Corinthians 6:19–20. What perspective on our bodies does Paul teach in these verses? How would you explain this in your own words?

Day Four

Read 1 Corinthians 6:15–16. Again referring to sexual immorality, Paul points out what's most wrong about it. What is that? What does this explanation mean to you?

Day Five

Read 1 Corinthians 6:15–16. In the last phrase of verse 16, Paul quotes from Genesis 2:24, which was written in reference to the creation of Adam and Eve and their marriage. In your understanding, what does this "oneness" in marriage include?

Last Session

We discussed the twist that the devil has placed on our pain. And in doing so we saw the big picture — past, present, and future — of how we're broken people in a broken world, but with the soon-coming hope of liberation and salvation. This week we turn to the deception that has been placed on sex.

SESSION 5

IT'S ONLY PHYSICAL

What the Bible has to say about sex is not only true; it's good, common-sense advice.

Even if you don't believe in the Bible's authority on the subject, as old-fashioned and impractical as it may sound sometimes, it's still incredibly relevant and worth talking about. And ultimately, in the hearts of most people, there's something about it that rings true.

Even if you don't bring the Bible into it, just take a look at the approach to sex our culture constantly promotes. Is it working? Are we better off? Are we happier? Are children healthier and more wholesome? Are marriages lasting longer? Are more families staying together? Has it even helped the economy?

The answer of course is no. You know it's not working. Having bought our culture's lie about sex, we're paying the price every single day. And the real rip-off for a young man or young woman making poor sexual choices is that their worst impact isn't felt in those young years, but in the next stages of life.

What God says about sex is radically different than what our culture promotes. Why? Because, while our culture's just living a lie, God *loves* you.

So let's face up to this. Let's not pretend anymore.

DISCUSSION STARTER

What do you see as the strongest messages about sex that our culture conveys today? How does it get these messages across, and how effective do they seem to be? In what ways has your own view of sex been shaped by the culture around you?

VIDEO OVERVIEW

FOR SESSION 5 OF THE DVD

Sex is for married people only. How absurd is that?

Not for any consenting adult, or anybody ready for it — but *married* people.

Sex outside marriage doesn't lead anywhere good. Nobody looks back and says, "Gosh, if I'd only slept with more people! If only I'd had more different kinds of sex! If I'd only experimented more!" We don't hear that, because it would be a lie.

So, what's wrong? How can something so obvious be so ignored? Why does it come across so laughable to say, "Sex is for married people only"?

Because our view of sex is so twisted. We think of sex as an activity, an event, something physical that you do. But the Bible tells us that sex is a soul thing, a heart thing. It's God's way to illustrate and create a sense of intimacy. When we take this incredible gift of sex and rip it out of the context God designed it for — marriage — then we foul up our intimacy factor. It damages our ability to be intimate.

In the New Testament, Paul wrote to the Corinthians, who lived in a culture where sex was viewed as only an activity. Paul told them, "Flee from sexual immorality" (1 Corinthians 6:18). What exactly is "sexual immorality"? In the Bible, sexual immorality is *any sexuality or intentional sensuality outside the context of marriage.* And Paul says we're to run away from it.

He tells us that sexual sin is unique; it's in a category all its own: "All other sins a man commits are outside his body, but he who sins sexually sins against his own body" (6:18). The consequences of sexual sin are different. Why is that?

It's because, Paul reminds us, sex is *oneness*: it unites two people, and the union is permanent. He refers back to what was written about the creation of Adam and Eve: "The two will become one flesh" (6:16; Genesis 2:24). After sex together, even if you abandon each other later, both people take a part of the other with them. It is not an isolated event, and it will forever impact your ability to experience intimacy.

And while our culture never discusses these issues, deep inside, we know the truth. We know the impact that this twist can have on us. And if we ever want to experience all that God has for us in this area, we must listen to what God has said. He designed sex. He gave us this gift. We need to stop believing the twist our culture has accepted and start understanding the importance of the truth about sex.

VIDEO NOTES

_____

_____

_____

_____

_____

_____

_____

_____

_____

_____

_____

_____

_____

_____

_____

_____

_____

_____

DISCUSSION QUESTIONS

1. What does our culture say about sex?

2. How is our culture's view of sex twisted?

3. According to your understanding of the Bible, what is God's purpose for sex?

4. First Corinthians 6:16 states that sex unites two to become one flesh. What is the impact of this kind of union?

5. Why does 1 Corinthians 6:18 say that sexual sin is different from other sins?

6. How will you *flee from sexual immorality* and honor God with your body?

MILEPOSTS

*   Sex is not merely an activity or event (as our culture insists), but rather God's way of illustrating and creating oneness and intimacy exclusively in marriage.
*   Sex outside marriage not only violates God's design and purpose, but it also brings long-term damage to our capacity for intimacy. In this sense, sexual sin is different from all other sin. Its harmful effects are deep and lasting.

MOVING FORWARD

Knowing the potential power and beauty of sex in the right context of marriage, according to God's guidelines, the devil has chosen to push hard in deceiving our culture with the pervasiveness and intensity of unhealthy sexuality. Is there currently any sexual immorality in your life, in any form? If so, make your decision to flee from it immediately, in obedience to God's command. Write down the steps of action you must take.

CHANGING YOUR MIND

Meditate on this simple but profound phrase from God's Word this week — as you face the barrage of our culture's twisted messages about sex.

Flee from sexual immorality.

1 Corinthians 6:18

PREPARATION FOR SESSION 6

To help you prepare for Session 6, use these suggested devotions during the week leading up to your small group meeting.

Day One

The last twist of the devil that we will cover in this guide has to do with sin. To start off we are going to turn to the Sermon on the Mount and begin to look at what Jesus had to say about following God. Read the words of Jesus in Matthew 5:17–19. From what he says here, is there any indication that he came to earth to do away with Old Testament laws, and make things a bit easier for those who follow God? What was his perspective on the Old Testament? And why might that be important for us to know?

Day Two

Read Matthew 5:20. In that culture, the Pharisees were considered to be the holiest and most religious people around. According to what Jesus says here, how should that compare with all the rest of us? (The word *righteousness* in this verse means "right living.")

Day Three

Read the words of Jesus in Matthew 5:21–22 and 5:27–28. How

is Jesus raising the standards for what it means to please God and avoid sin? How does your own life compare to these higher standards?

Day Four

Read the words of Jesus in Matthew 5:31–32. In Old Testament times, a man could divorce his wife — giving her "a certificate of divorce" — for practically any reason. What different perspective does Jesus teach here? How do his words compare to your own view of divorce?

Day Five

Read Matthew 5:43–48. Again, how is Jesus raising the standards for what it means to please God? What is the ultimate standard that Jesus says we must attain? Who can attain this standard?

Last Session

We saw that sex outside marriage — as actively promoted by our twisted culture — not only violates God's design but also brings long-term damage to our capacity for intimacy. Sex isn't just an activity (as our culture says), but God's way of illustrating and creating oneness and intimacy in marriage. This week we turn to the important concept of sin.

IT'S NO MISTAKE

Sin. It's such a pesky word. And we don't use it much.

Imagine getting pulled over by a policeman for speeding, and as he steps up to your car window he announces, "You've sinned." Or you mess up a project at work, so your boss calls you into his office and tells you, "You sinned against the company." Or you get a letter from the IRS that begins, "You are guilty of sin against the government."

Not likely. We don't use the S-word. We don't like it.

And no wonder. It doesn't make us feel good about ourselves. Sin makes us think of being accountable to God and his judgment and punishment. It brings to mind divine law and moral absolutes and (as the dictionary puts it) "a willful or deliberate violation" of them. It implies we need forgiveness — and that we'll have to *ask* for it.

There's another term we like a lot better: "I just made a mistake." That's all. *Okay, so I made a mistake. Nobody's perfect! Can we just move on?* No punishment required, no forgiveness.

Yes, there's a big, big difference between *mistake* and *sin*. Let's get straight on exactly what that difference is.

DISCUSSION STARTER

Over the last couple of weeks, what are some mistakes that you have made? What were the circumstances or assumptions that caused those mistakes?

VIDEO OVERVIEW

FOR SESSION 6 OF THE DVD

The biggest difference between "sin" and "just a mistake" is this: If my wrongdoing is only a mistake, that makes me merely a *mistaker*. Without *sin*, I'm not a *sinner* — and have no need for a savior.

If I'm just a mistaker (as the twist in today's culture tells us), all I need to do is try harder next time. Just break those nasty little habits. Be more consistent, more disciplined, more committed.

But if I'm a sinner, that's more fundamental to who I am. Trying harder won't cut it. If I'm a sinner, I need a savior.

If we're honest with ourselves, we can see through the twist. We do wrong and know exactly what we're doing. It isn't careless or unintentional. We may fool others, but not ourselves.

There's also the matter of our disturbing thoughts. No one else sees them, but we can't escape their repulsiveness.

And what about the guilt we feel? It's deep and dark — and it's real, not imagined.

As if all that wasn't enough, starting in Matthew 5, Jesus raises the standard on how good we must be in God's eyes. Jesus says that an angry word is like murder and a lustful thought like adultery. He says we must love and pray for our enemies. He says our righteousness — the right kind of living — must surpass anything we've witnessed in others.

Seeing such standards, we respond, "Then there's nobody righteous but God!"

Jesus says, "That's my point." And that's why we need a savior.

In the teachings of Jesus, we encounter two very opposing ideas: "God loves you," and "You sin; you're a sinner." Which is it?

"It's both," Jesus tells us. "You're a sinner—but God loves you. You're worse than you thought, but God loves you more than you imagined." In that love, he provides the Savior from our sin — Jesus, his Son.

Otherwise, there's no hope for us. We'll never be able to overcome our sin and meet God's standards through our own efforts.

We need a savior.

VIDEO NOTES

_____

_____

_____

_____

_____

_____

_____

_____

_____

_____

_____

_____

_____

_____

_____

_____

_____

_____

_____

DISCUSSION QUESTIONS

1. How have you seen the meaning of sin twisted by our culture?

2. Romans 3:23 makes it clear that everyone has sinned. While most people would agree that nobody is perfect, what is at stake when people buy into the twist and fail to realize the sinfulness that lies at their cores? Do you know people who have bought into this twist?

3. What was Jesus' message concerning sin from his statements in Matthew 5? What are the different ways that his message affected people? What effect does it have on you?

4. What did God do in response to our sin?

5. Have you come to realize that you are a *sinner* rather than a *mistaker*? If so, when did this happen?

MILEPOSTS

- Our culture teaches us to view wrongdoing as "just a mistake" rather than as sin.
- Buying into this twist blinds us to our true need for a savior.
- Jesus teaches us not only that we're worse sinners than we thought, but that God loves us more than we can imagine. In that amazing love, Jesus is our Savior from sin.

MOVING FORWARD

The gospel of Jesus Christ is "good news" because of the "bad news" of our sin and its consequences. Have you embraced the reality that you're a sinner who needs the Savior?

If so, express again (in a written prayer) your gratitude to God for providing your salvation through the death of Jesus Christ, his Son. Learn to pay special attention to thanking God for this gift as often as you can.

If you have *not* previously embraced the fact that you're a sinner who needs a Savior, but you want to do that now, you can pray something like this (or use your own words to express your new faith in Christ):

"God, I'm not just a mistaker; I'm a sinner. I've sinned against you, and I owe you a debt I can't pay. I believe that when Jesus died on the cross, he paid that debt for my sin. Today, I'm personally receiving your free gift of salvation and your forgiveness of my sin. I no longer trust my own abilities and efforts; instead, I trust the work that Christ completed for me on the cross."

That's how sinners find forgiveness and enter the kingdom of God!

CHANGING YOUR MIND

This statement from Jesus' Sermon on the Mount is a good reminder of why we need a Savior. Your loving Savior himself is telling you this … and he ultimately makes it possible for you, through your faith in him:

> *Be perfect, therefore,*
> *as your heavenly Father is perfect.*
>
> *Matthew 5:48*

LEADER'S GUIDE

So, You're the Leader...

Is that intimidating? Perhaps exciting? No doubt you have some mental pictures of what it will look like, what you will say, and how it will go. Before you get too far into the planning process, there are some things you should know about leading a small group discussion. We've compiled some tried and true techniques here to help you.

BASICS ABOUT LEADING

1. Cultivate discussion — It's also easy to think that the meeting lives or dies by your ideas. In reality, what makes a small-group meeting successful are the ideas of everyone in the group. The most valuable thing you can do is to get people to share their thoughts. That's how the relationships in your group will grow and thrive. Here's a rule: The impact of your study material will typically never exceed the impact of the relationships through which it was studied. The more meaningful the relationships, the more meaningful the study. In a sterile environment, even the best material is suppressed.

2. **Point to the material** — A good host or hostess gets the party going by offering delectable hors d'oeuvres and beverages. You too should be ready to serve up "delicacies" from the material. Sometimes you will simply read the discussion questions and invite everyone to respond. At other times, you may encourage others to share their ideas. Remember, some of the best treats are the ones your guests will bring to the party. Go with the flow of the meeting, and be ready to pop out of the kitchen as needed.

3. **Depart from the material** — A talented ministry team has carefully designed this study for your small group. But that doesn't mean you should follow every part word for word. Knowing how and when to depart from the material is a valuable art. Nobody knows more about your people than you do. The narratives, questions, and exercises are here to provide a framework for discovery. However, every group is motivated differently. Sometimes the best way to start a small group discussion is simply to ask, "Does anyone have a personal insight or revelation he'd like to share from this week's material?" Then sit back and listen.

4. **Stay on track** — Conversation is like the currency of a small-group discussion. The more interchange, the healthier the "econo-

my." However, you need to keep your objectives in mind. If your goal is to have a meaningful experience with this material, then you should make sure the discussion is contributing to that end. It's easy to get off on a tangent. Be prepared to interject politely and refocus the group. You may need to say something like, "Excuse me, we're obviously all interested in this subject; however, I just want to make sure we cover all the material for this week."

5. Above all, pray — The best communicators are the ones that manage to get out of God's way enough to let him communicate *through* them. That's important to keep in mind. Books don't teach God's Word; neither do sermons or group discussions. God himself speaks into the hearts of men and women, and prayer is our vital channel to communicate directly with him. Cover your efforts in prayer. You don't just want God present at your meeting, you want him to direct it.

We hope you find these suggestions helpful. And we hope you enjoy leading this study. You will find additional guidelines and suggestions for each session in the Leader's Guide notes that follow.

LEADER'S GUIDE SESSION NOTES

SESSION 1 - THE SOURCE OF DECEPTION

Bottom Line

As Jesus makes clear, the devil is a murderer and a liar. His goal is the destruction of human life, and his tool for doing this is *deception*. The entire world — each and every one of us — is subject to his destructive, deceptive influence.

Discussion Starter

You can take a lighthearted approach here. The stories of how each person has fallen for something are likely to be amusing. (Be sure to tell one about yourself.) The second part of this exercise — the question about how susceptible to deception they consider themselves to be — should be interesting and revealing.

Notes for Discussion Questions

1. **In what ways are you affected by things you can't see (e.g., germs, electricity, the wind, etc.)?**

   Use this easy question to get everyone comfortable with talking and sharing with each other. Where appropriate, encourage humor in their responses to help "break the ice" further and warm up the group.

2. **How does our culture portray the devil?**

   Their answers will probably include the observation that many in our culture definitely do not believe in the reality of the devil. Ask them why this is the case.

3. **What is your understanding of who the devil is?**

   The discussion may be slow to start, since many in your group may have given little serious thought to the devil. Mention that possibility, and ask why this could be the case with many of us. (This is the first discussion question in this study that focuses on each group member's personal answers on a significant issue.) Spend enough time to allow everyone to share fully. This will help set a good precedent for open and honest sharing.

4. **What do we learn about the devil from Jesus in John 8:43–44?**

   Do they see each point that Jesus brings out in this session's Scripture verses? Help draw their attention to any points they miss or fail to grasp.

5. **Read Luke 4:5–6. Does it surprise you that God has granted the devil temporary influence on the world around us? Why would God allow this?**

   Especially for those whose answers are "yes," draw out the reasons behind their responses. Don't shy away from exploring the tensions between (a) God's ultimate control of all things, (b) the devil's empowered influence in this world, and (c) our own individual wills and responsible actions. Emphasize the practical, experiential impact of the devil's work.

6. **How has the devil's influence been felt in this world?**

   The wider picture of this will be explored in Session 2, but your group may already begin to grasp the tragic dimensions of the devil's influence. Not a happy picture! But it is a true and present reality.

Moving Forward

The goal is to help everyone attain the correct biblical balance regarding the devil's powers and not lose sight of Christ's infinite superiority to him. This assurance helps break down the resistance many of us have to this subject and helps us instead to assess more realistically the acute dangers of the devil's influence.

Preparation for Session 2

Remember to point out the brief daily devotions which the group members can complete and which will help greatly in stimulating discussion in your next session. These devotions will enable everyone to dig into the Bible and start wrestling with the topics that will come up next time.

SESSION 2 – ALL IS NOT AS IT SEEMS

Bottom Line

The devil's destructive and deceptive strategy includes many twist-ings of truth which inevitably bring struggles into our lives. The devil's destructive and deceptive assault against humanity is the only valid explanation for the degree of evil we see in our world.

Discussion Starter

Every day we likely hear twists in the truth when we are listening to all that is going on around us. Help group members pick out some truths they have heard lately that have been twisted.

Notes for Discussion Questions

1. **From your observations, how has our world been af-fected by twisted thinking?**

   Encourage everyone to identify some of the worst effects of twisted thinking.

2. **How have you fallen victim to twisted thinking in the past? Are there times when you've looked back**

and asked, "What was I thinking?" How were you led astray?

Openness and honesty in their answers will depend on the group dynamics and their comfort with each other. Giving a candid and unflattering answer yourself will help the others share more freely.

3. **If it's not because of an evil entity called the devil, how do people account for twisted thinking?**

There could be a wide variety of answers. You may want to encourage them to give examples from their own lives, past and present, of such twists apart from any reference to the devil.

4. **Read Ephesians 6:12. Do you agree that we struggle not only against what we can see, but also against unseen forces? How does this fact affect some of the current conflicts you're experiencing?**

Most of us would normally prefer not to focus right now on our personal conflicts and struggles (don't we do that enough already?). But making the personal connection to the truths being taught in these early sessions is the key to having a healthy, biblical, balanced understanding of the hardships and conflicts we all face in life. Again, your own example of honest sharing can be powerful and encouraging for the others.

5. **According to Ephesians 6:13–17, how can you protect yourself from twisted thinking?**

   Look especially to biblical perspectives and principles — in particular those found throughout Ephesians 6:10–18. These teachings may already be well-known to some in your group, but when we view more realistically the personal impact of the devil's schemes against us, these biblical principles and promises become real in a new way. As these recognitions are made, this may be a good time to pray together in response.

Moving Forward

To begin praying these prayers consistently is a giant step forward in freedom from the devil's deceptions. These are prayers God loves to answer! The exercises listed should help everyone articulate the bigger perspective that's been presented in Sessions 1 and 2, and to relate it personally to the very real struggles in their own lives.

Preparation for Session 3

Again, encourage your group members to complete the brief daily devotions. These will help stimulate discussion in your next session. They'll enable everyone to dig into the Bible and start wrestling with the topics coming up next time.

SESSION 3 - SAYS WHO?

Bottom Line

Our normal (and twisted) response to authority is to first evaluate everything we're asked to do, then submit only to what we agree with. But the Bible teaches us that God has established human authorities as agents of his own will. So resisting or disobeying the human authorities God has established is ultimately rebellion against God himself.

Discussion Starter

We've all been here. There could be plenty of laughter as the stories come out. Meanwhile, the last question in this exercise might help point the group to a little more seriousness in examining our deep-rooted resistance to authority.

Notes for Discussion Questions

1. **What rules or regulations do you disagree with? Do you follow them or ignore them?**

   Probably everyone in the group has some area of life where authority is resisted and rules are broken. So take the lead in being honest.

2. **What determines whether or not you submit to authority and follow the rules?**

    Encourage all group memebers to analyze the mental processes behind their responses to authority. You may hear some surprising rationalizations, faulty assumptions, and intricate excuses. Be sure the group understands that this isn't an investigation to expose wrong behavior; it's simply a starter for thought and discussion.

3. **Does it surprise you that according to Romans 13:1, all authorities have been set up by God? How about the authorities that don't follow God?**

    There may be resistance to this statement from some in the group, especially when considering abusive and corrupt authorities — of which there are obviously many. You may want to bring in the biblical pattern of responding to unjust authorities by appealing to the next higher authority — ultimately going all the way up to God in prayer.

4. **What is at stake when we choose to rebel?**

    This is a key recognition. Help everyone focus on the implications in Romans 13:1–7 of what's at stake.

5. **What is the purpose of authority? Why not live in a world with no rules or hierarchy?**

    Here again, Romans 13:1–7 points us in the right direction. Encourage the group to think in terms of what God is trying to accomplish for our good.

6. **What are some ways you could experience more freedom by submitting to authority?**

    This should tie in closely with answers to the previous question. As God's wisdom and grace and love for us become clearer in how he's placed authorities over us, take time to pray together, offering praise and gratitude to your heavenly Father.

Moving Forward

It's vitally important to have a compelling picture in mind of the value of submitting to human authorities. By doing so, we'll ultimately please not only God, but also ourselves!

Encourage everyone to be genuinely prayerful in deciding what action steps to take and then to be very specific in writing them down.

Preparation for Session 4

Again, encourage your group members to complete the daily devotions. This will help them be better prepared for the topics coming up next time.

SESSION 4 - FACING FORWARD

Bottom Line

We live in a broken world that's in bondage to sin, death, and decay — all as a result of humanity's first rebellion against God. In this life we cannot escape those things; life on this earth is in many ways a downward spiral. But we can look forward in hope to a future when we'll experience complete liberation and salvation. Meanwhile, through his Spirit, God helps us in our weakness as we wait eagerly for what's ahead.

Discussion Starter

We all experience pain and suffering in our lives. Help group members pick out one or two experiences that they have had lately. Make sure you are also open and honest.

Notes for Discussion Questions

1. **Why do we tend to believe the twist that the reason for our pain can be found in past events or present circumstances?**

   This kind of response to pain and suffering is so universal and deep-rooted that it can be hard to see past it. Why do we ask why? It may seem unsearchable. But as everyone pushes deep, insights and recognitions will start to emerge.

2. **When have you tried to do this only to end up frustrated? That is, when have you experienced pain, or watched as others experienced pain, that seemed to have no purpose?**

   Allow plenty of time for personal sharing, and set a good example of attentive, sensitive listening. Give everyone the freedom to express the kind of emotions that necessarily arise when we encounter what seems to be meaningless suffering.

3. **According to Romans 8:18, we are to hold our present suffering in light of a more hopeful future. But how has the pain in your life affected your present relationship with God? Has it made you more dependent on him? Or has it pushed you away and made you more independent? How have you seen suffering affect the faith of those around you?**

   Again, don't rush the time in answering this intensely personal question. There may be deep fears that hold some back from the freedom to be honest about this. It's critically important to refrain from expressing any judgments upon the doubts and struggles shared by others in the group.

4. **In the beginning, God created a paradise (Genesis 1); however, when we rebelled, sin, death, and decay entered the world (Genesis 3). How does "the beginning" relate to your understanding of the pain you've experienced?**

   Although making this connection is not emotionally satisfying for us — or even intellectually satisfying — it still brings us closer to something our souls deeply long for. In your discussion together, can you identify what this is?

5. **Romans 8:26–28 addresses the Spirit's work in our weakness. How does the Spirit help us "in the meantime"? How does God provide help for us during times of suffering?**

   Dive into Romans 8:26–28 to enjoy the refreshment of these positive affirmations of the Spirit's help. You'll welcome this positive shift after the heaviness of the previous questions.

6. **How does knowing what lies ahead "in the meantime" affect our present suffering?**

   Tragically, many do not make this connection and experience the hope that can truly be ours in even the worst suffering. If those in your group do get it, that's a wonderful manifestation of God's grace in their lives. Make sure you pause to express your gratefulness for this grace.

Moving Forward

Actively expressing our hope (or lack of it) in open communication with the Lord is crucial. As we turn our inward focus on him, he'll be faithful to lift up our hearts in true hope and peace and joy. Most of us have a long way to go in developing a more vibrant hope. Having a realistic picture of where we currently are on that score can help motivate us to move forward to more intensity of hope. It can help us see more clearly our negativity and anxiety, so we can break free from that. God wants us to be hopeful and cheerful in our overall experience of life, not gloomy and weighed down.

Preparation for Session 5

Again, encourage your group members to complete the daily devotions, helping them be better prepared for the topics coming up next time.

SESSION 5 – IT'S ONLY PHYSICAL

Bottom Line

Sex is not merely an activity or event (as our twisted culture insists), but rather God's way of illustrating and creating oneness and intimacy exclusively in marriage. The Bible teaches us to completely avoid any sexuality or intentional sensuality outside the context of marriage, because it not only violates God's design and purpose, but also brings long-term damage to our capacity for intimacy. In this sense, sexual sin is different from all other sin. Its harmful effects are deep and lasting.

Discussion Starter

Everyone's answers to the last question should be interesting — how has our own view of sex been shaped by the culture around us? Some who view themselves as independent thinkers may think they haven't been influenced at all by culture in this regard. But a little probing might well reveal otherwise.

Notes for Discussion Questions

1.   **What does our culture say about sex?**

     There's no shortage of things to mention here! (Responses
     to this question may overlap with the discussion starter.
     Just pick up where you left off. Or if you think this has
     been covered enough already, move on to the next ques-
     tion.)

2.   **How is our culture's view of sex twisted?**

     Likewise here, there's plenty to expose. But some in the
     group may not fully recognize the twists that are all around
     us. Explore this carefully.

3.   **According to your understanding of the Bible, what is
     God's purpose for sex?**

     This is important to discuss fully. You may want to ac-
     knowledge how much God is "for" sex, not against it. It
     is, in fact, the high value that he places on sex that brings
     his warnings about misapplying it. He loves us enough to
     insist on our best experience of sex.

4. **First Corinthians 6:16 states that sex unites two to become one flesh. What is the impact of this kind of union?**

What's key is seeing how sex is so linked to our capacity for intimacy. That's why sexual immorality brings serious long-term damage to that capacity. Be sensitive to the likelihood that some in your group may still feel the effects of this damage because of sexual immorality that occurred years or even decades ago —possibly through no responsibility of their own (as when children are sexually molested). It may be difficult or impossible at this point for them to talk about it openly in your group. Be sensitive to this reality — and to the fact that this discussion can be a step forward in healing for them.

5. **Why does 1 Corinthians 6:18 say that sexual sin is different from other sins?**

Take notice of the profound statements about this in 1 Corinthians 6:15–20.

6. **How will you flee from sexual immorality and honor God with your body?**

    On such a sensitive issue, some may hesitate to answer this question, even if they have a clear plan and intention for making a turnaround in obedience to God. You may want to offer encouragement by mentioning several examples of positive steps of obedience in this area.

Moving Forward

This exercise is meant to deepen everyone's grasp of the vast, infinite chasm between God's exalted view of sex and the devil's distortion of it. Encourage everyone to be genuinely prayerful in deciding what action steps to take and then to be very specific in writing them down.

Preparation for Session 6

Once more, encourage your group members to complete the daily devotions in preparation for the next session.

SESSION 6 – IT'S NO MISTAKE

Bottom Line

Our culture teaches us to view wrongdoing as "just a mistake" rather than as sin. Buying into this twist blinds us to our true need for a savior. But Jesus opens our eyes to the facts: We're not only worse sinners than we thought, but God loves us more than we can imagine! In that amazing love, Jesus is our Savior from sin.

Discussion Starter

We all make mistakes, so start the discussion off by helping people identify some of the mistakes they have made lately.

Notes for Discussion Questions

1. **How have you seen the meaning of sin twisted by our culture?**

    Some may observe that the word sin is mostly absent in today's culture. That says a lot right there!

2. **Romans 3:23 makes it clear that everyone has sinned. While most people would agree that nobody is perfect,**

what is at stake when people buy into the twist and fail to realize the sinfulness that lies at their core? Do you know people who have bought into this twist?

The key observation here is that ultimately our felt need for a savior disappears when sin disappears from our consciousness.

3. **What was Jesus' message concerning sin from his statements in Matthew 5? What are the different ways that his message affected people? What effect does it have on you?**

Look throughout Matthew 5:17–48 to explore Jesus' message and to consider the reactions to it. Some in the group may think of other teachings from Jesus to mention as well.

4. **What did God do in response to our sin?**

Listen clearly to all the answers to discover how well they comprehend the gospel. Nothing is more critical for us to understand than this. A few gospel statements from the Bible that you may want to glance at together include John 3:16, Romans 5:8–11, Ephesians 2:1–10, and 1 Timothy 2:5–6.

5. **Have you come to realize that you are a sinner rather than a mistaker? If so, when did this happen?**

    To get beyond simple "yes" or "no" answers, discuss more fully why it can be so difficult to admit we're sinners. Help everyone to recognize these obstacles — which is the first step to overcoming them.

Moving Forward

We've looked at a lot of "bad news" in this study. Now help ensure that this translates into a corresponding greater appreciation of the good news of Jesus Christ and our salvation in him. This exercise can help articulate that.

Encourage all group memebers to focus their attention and gratitude on God's gift to us of salvation through the death and resurrection of his Son, Jesus Christ. It's impossible to thank him too much or too often, for the gospel reveals God's infinite goodness and grace and justice and love.

As the leader, be particularly encouraging and helpful for anyone in the group who's new to faith.

Share Your Thoughts

With the Author: Your comments will be forwarded to
the author when you send them to *zauthor@zondervan.com*.

With Zondervan: Submit your review of this book
by writing to *zreview@zondervan.com*.

Free Online Resources at
www.zondervan.com/hello

 Zondervan AuthorTracker: Be notified whenever your
favorite authors publish new books, go on tour, or post
an update about what's happening in their lives.

 Daily Bible Verses and Devotions: Enrich your life
with daily Bible verses or devotions that help you start
every morning focused on God.

 Free Email Publications: Sign up for newsletters on
fiction, Christian living, church ministry, parenting, and
more.

 Zondervan Bible Search: Find and compare
Bible passages in a variety of translations at
www.zondervanbiblesearch.com.

 Other Benefits: Register yourself to receive online
benefits like coupons and special offers, or to participate
in research.